# MY FIRST
# WORLD
# ATLAS

# EUROPE

Europe is the second smallest continent in the world, yet has the second largest population. It contains over 40 countries, each with its own government and capital city.

## FACTS

- Europe covers 7% of the world's land surface

- Highest point is Mount Elbrus in the Caucasus mountain range

- The Vatican City (just 0.44sq.km) is Europe's, and the world's, smallest country

Norwegian Sea

NORWAY

Oslo ●

SWEDEN

NORTHERN IRELAND

SCOTLAND

North Sea

IRELAND

ENGLAND

DENMARK

Baltic Sea

WALES

London ●

Atlantic Ocean

HOLLAND

BELGIUM

GERMANY

LUXEMBOURG

Paris ●

CZECH REPUBLIC

LIECHTENSTEIN

Bay of Biscay

FRANCE

SWITZERLAND

AUSTRIA

SLOVENIA

ITALY

CROATIA

PORTUGAL

SPAIN

BOSNIA

Madrid ●

MONTENEGRO

Rome ●

CORSICA

BALEARIC ISLANDS

SARDINIA

Mediterranean Sea

SICILY

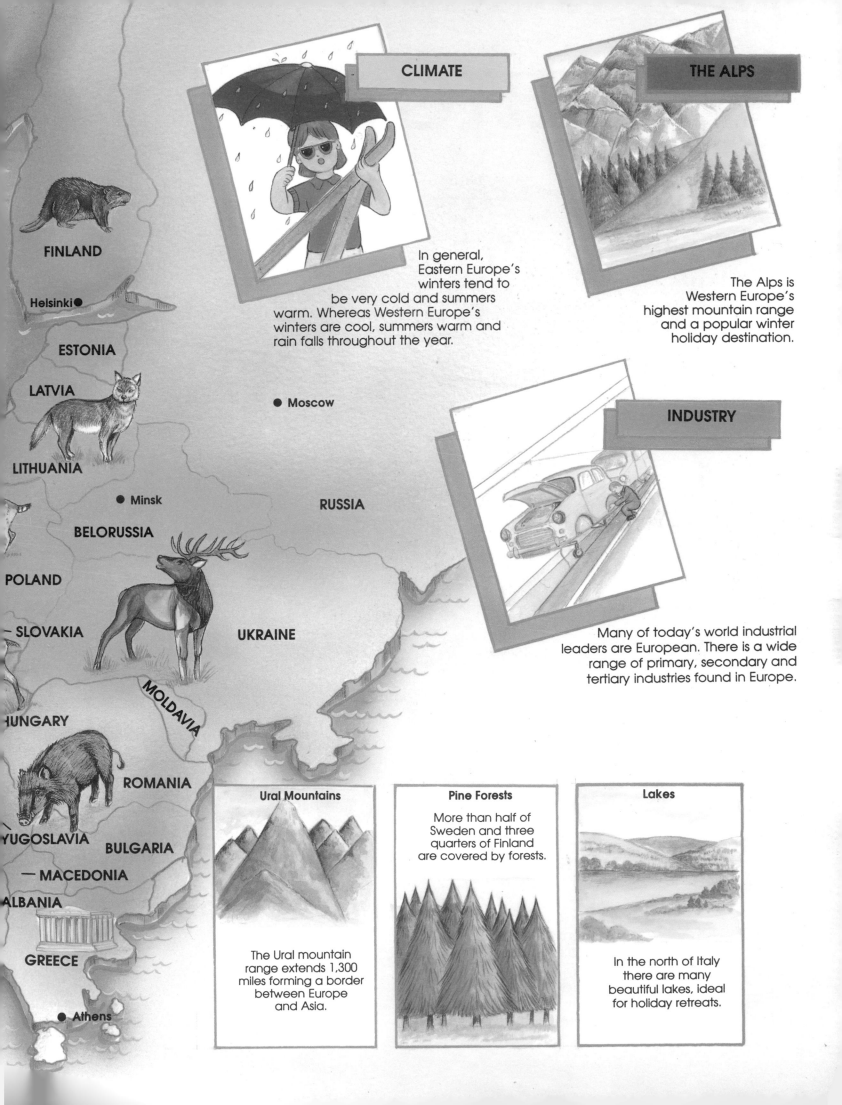

FINLAND

Helsinki●

ESTONIA

LATVIA

LITHUANIA

● Minsk

BELORUSSIA

POLAND

— SLOVAKIA

HUNGARY

ROMANIA

YUGOSLAVIA

BULGARIA

— MACEDONIA

ALBANIA

GREECE

● Athens

MOLDAVIA

UKRAINE

● Moscow

RUSSIA

## CLIMATE

In general, Eastern Europe's winters tend to be very cold and summers warm. Whereas Western Europe's winters are cool, summers warm and rain falls throughout the year.

## THE ALPS

The Alps is Western Europe's highest mountain range and a popular winter holiday destination.

## INDUSTRY

Many of today's world industrial leaders are European. There is a wide range of primary, secondary and tertiary industries found in Europe.

### Ural Mountains

The Ural mountain range extends 1,300 miles forming a border between Europe and Asia.

### Pine Forests

More than half of Sweden and three quarters of Finland are covered by forests.

### Lakes

In the north of Italy there are many beautiful lakes, ideal for holiday retreats.

# AFRICA

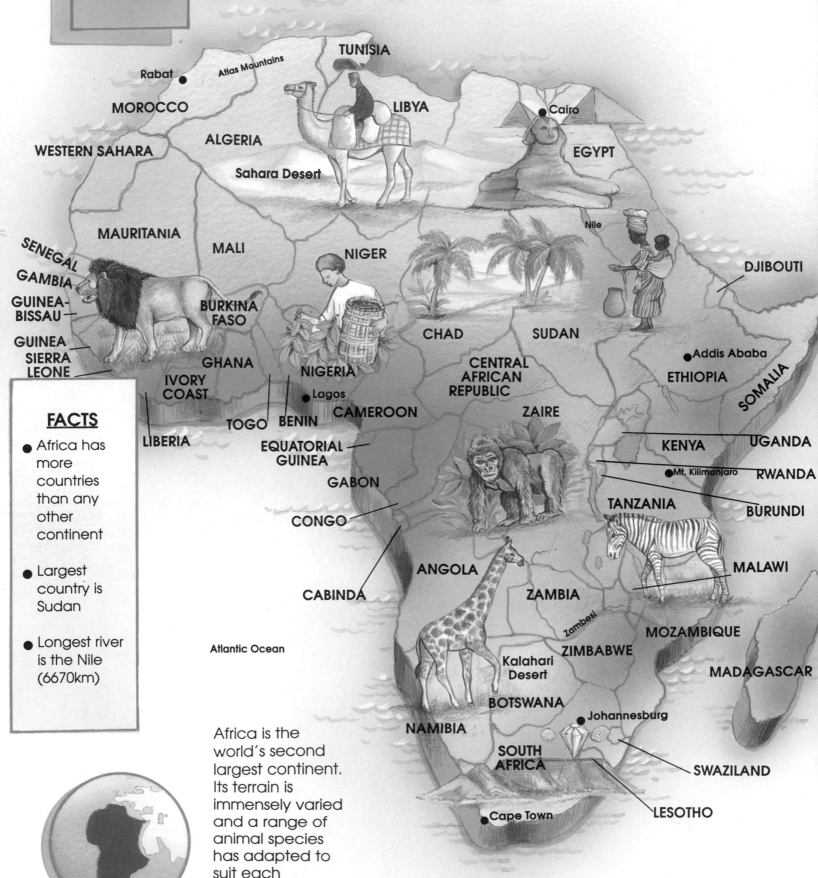

Rabat •
MOROCCO
Atlas Mountains
TUNISIA
LIBYA
Cairo •
EGYPT
WESTERN SAHARA
ALGERIA
Sahara Desert
Nile
MAURITANIA
MALI
NIGER
DJIBOUTI
SENEGAL
GAMBIA
BURKINA
FASO
CHAD
SUDAN
Addis Ababa •
ETHIOPIA
SOMALIA
GUINEA-
BISSAU
GUINEA
SIERRA
LEONE
GHANA
CENTRAL
AFRICAN
REPUBLIC
IVORY
COAST
NIGERIA
ZAIRE
KENYA
UGANDA
Mt. Kilimanjaro •
RWANDA
LIBERIA
TOGO
BENIN
CAMEROON
Lagos •
EQUATORIAL
GUINEA
GABON
TANZANIA
BURUNDI
CONGO
MALAWI
ANGOLA
CABINDA
ZAMBIA
MOZAMBIQUE
Zambesi
ZIMBABWE
MADAGASCAR
Kalahari
Desert
Atlantic Ocean
BOTSWANA
Johannesburg •
NAMIBIA
SOUTH
AFRICA
SWAZILAND
LESOTHO
Cape Town •

## FACTS

- Africa has more countries than any other continent
- Largest country is Sudan
- Longest river is the Nile (6670km)

Africa is the world's second largest continent. Its terrain is immensely varied and a range of animal species has adapted to suit each environment.

## DESERT

In North Africa is the Sahara Desert, the largest area of dry land in the world. Covering approximately 9 million sq.km., only one sixth is sandy, the rest rocky or stoney.

## RAINFOREST

In central Africa, around the Equator, there are dense tropical rainforests, typical of the hot and wet equatorial climate.

**Mount Kilimanjaro**

Lying just south of the Equator in Tanzania, Mount Kilimanjaro stands as the highest point of Africa at 5895m.

Much of East Africa is covered by savannah, or grasslands, and here are found some of the world's largest herds of wild game.

**Savannah**

**Victoria Falls**

On the border between Zambia and Zimbabwe are the spectacular Victoria Falls of the Zambezi River.

# AUSTRALIA

Australia is a sparsely populated island divided into seven self-governing states. Its capital city is Canberra.

New Zealand is divided into North Island and South Island. Most of New Zealand's population live on North Island, in the cities of Auckland and Wellington.

Darwin

**NORTHERN TERRITORY**

**WESTERN AUSTRALIA**

**GREAT SANDY DESERT**

Alice Springs ●

Ayers Rock

**QUEENSLAND**

### FACTS

- Australia is the world's smallest continent

- Australia's largest city is Sydney

- Highest point is Mount Cook in New Zealand

**GREAT VICTORIA DESERT**

'Lake Eyre

● Perth

**SOUTH AUSTRALIA**

Darling

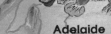

● Adelaide    Murr

**VICTORIA**

Melbo

● Auckland

**NEW ZEALAND**

● Wellington

● Christchurch

● Dunedin

## MANGROVE FOREST

Mangrove trees are tropical evergreens which have stilt-like intertwining roots. They form dense thickets on Australia's coasts.

## CORAL REEFS

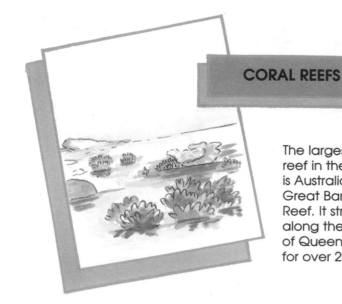

The largest coral reef in the world is Australia's Great Barrier Reef. It stretches along the coast of Queensland for over 2000kms.

Great Barrier Reef

Brisbane ●

EW SOUTH WALES

Sydney ●

● Canberra

**TASMANIA**

● Hobart

### Aboriginal Native

The Aborigines were the first inhabitants of Australia. They were nomadic hunters until displaced when Europeans arrived around 200 years ago.

### Sydney Harbour Bridge

Sydney Harbour Bridge is the city's chief landmark. It leads the way to the northern suberbs where most of Sydney's population live.

### World Famous Surfing

Some beaches in Australia are world famous for surfing and hold yearly competitions. Bells Beach in Victoria and the Gold Coast, New South Wales, are examples.

# NORTH AMERICA

North America stretches from the Arctic Circle to the Gulf of Mexico. It is the third largest continent and so wide it covers eight different time zones.

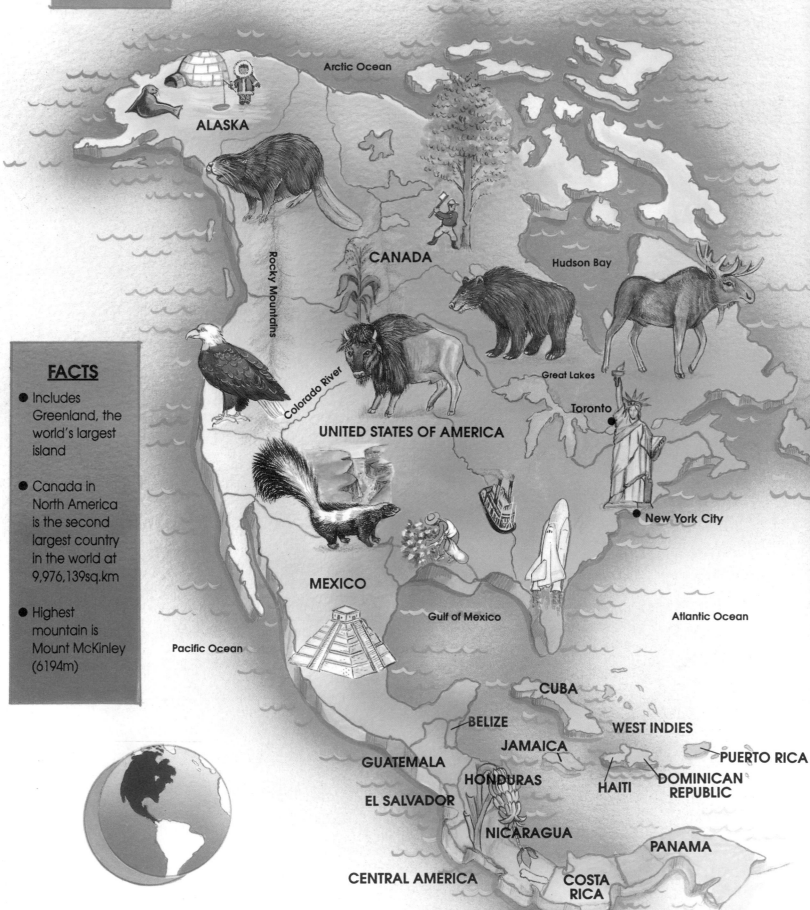

Arctic Ocean

ALASKA

CANADA

Hudson Bay

Rocky Mountains

Colorado River

UNITED STATES OF AMERICA

Great Lakes

Toronto

New York City

## FACTS

- Includes Greenland, the world's largest island

- Canada in North America is the second largest country in the world at 9,976,139sq.km

- Highest mountain is Mount McKinley (6194m)

MEXICO

Gulf of Mexico

Atlantic Ocean

Pacific Ocean

CUBA

BELIZE

WEST INDIES

JAMAICA

GUATEMALA

PUERTO RICA

HONDURAS

HAITI

DOMINICAN REPUBLIC

EL SALVADOR

NICARAGUA

PANAMA

CENTRAL AMERICA

COSTA RICA

## ROCKIES

The spectacular Rocky Mountains extend approximately 4800km from the Mexican border through the US and Canada to Alaska.

## PRAIRIES

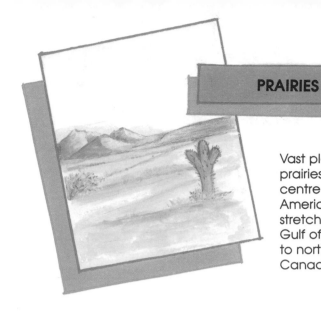

Vast plains, or prairies, lie at the centre of North America and stretch from the Gulf of Mexico to northern Canada.

### Tornados

Tornados are funnel-shaped storms that twist furiously up to 650km/hr. They occur mainly in the central states of the USA.

### Tropical South

Lying off the mainland are the islands of the West Indies, increasingly popular as holiday destinations.

### Skyscrapers

Skyscrapers are tall multi-storey buildings familiar in most large North American cities. The Manhatten skycraper skyline in New York is particularly famous.

# SOUTH AMERICA

South America has 13 countries, each with its own distinctive landscape and culture.

Caracas

VENEZUELA

GUYANA

SURINAM

FRENCH GUIANA

Orinoco River

COLOMBIA

Amazon River

ECUADOR

PERU

BRAZIL

Lima

Brasilia

La Paz

BOLIVIA

Rio De Janeiro

PARAGUAY

Sao Paulo

Pacific Ocean

CHILE

Parana River

URAGUAY

Santiago

Buenos Aires

ARGENTINA

Atlantic Ocean

Falkland Islands

Tierra Del Fuego

## FACTS

- The world's longest mountain range is the Andes, running over 8000km from North to South America

- Lake Titicaca on the border of Peru and Bolivia is the highest navigable lake in the world

- South America's largest city is Sao Paulo, Brazil

## AMAZON RAINFOREST

This is the largest tropical rainforest in the world. It is barely populated and has poor communications.

## PAMPAS GRASSLANDS

In Argentina there are flat grassland plains called pampas. They are mainly used for cattle and sheep grazing.

### Mount Aconcagua

Mount Aconcagua is the highest point (6960m) of Argentina and the Andes.

### Angel Falls in Canaima National Park

This spectacular waterfall in Veneuzuela is the highest in the world.

### Atacama Desert

The Atacama Desert in Chile contains some of the driest places on earth. Until 1971, parts were without rain for 400 years.

# ASIA

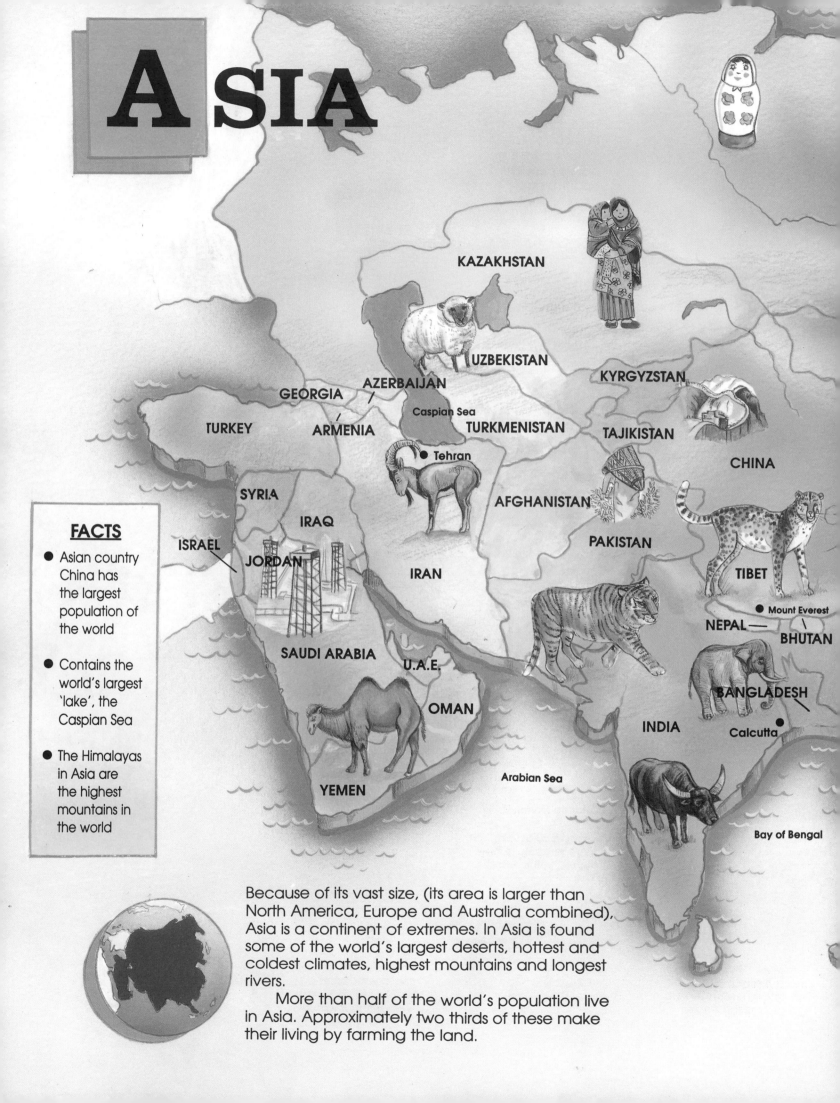

KAZAKHSTAN

UZBEKISTAN

KYRGYZSTAN

GEORGIA

AZERBAIJAN

Caspian Sea

TURKMENISTAN

TAJIKISTAN

CHINA

TURKEY

ARMENIA

• Tehran

SYRIA

AFGHANISTAN

IRAQ

PAKISTAN

TIBET

ISRAEL

JORDAN

IRAN

NEPAL — • Mount Everest

BHUTAN

SAUDI ARABIA

U.A.E.

BANGLADESH

OMAN

INDIA

• Calcutta

YEMEN

Arabian Sea

Bay of Bengal

## FACTS

- Asian country China has the largest population of the world

- Contains the world's largest 'lake', the Caspian Sea

- The Himalayas in Asia are the highest mountains in the world

Because of its vast size, (its area is larger than North America, Europe and Australia combined), Asia is a continent of extremes. In Asia is found some of the world's largest deserts, hottest and coldest climates, highest mountains and longest rivers.

More than half of the world's population live in Asia. Approximately two thirds of these make their living by farming the land.

RUSSIA

MONGOLIA

Huang He

NORTH KOREA

SOUTH KOREA

JAPAN

Chang Jiang

TAIWAN

Shanghai

JRMA

HONG KONG

HAILAND  LAOS

Bangkok

Manila

VIETNAM

PHILIPPINES

CAMBODIA

BRUNEI

MALAYSIA

BORNEO

INDONESIA

Pacific Ocean

## MONSOONS

The monsoon period of southern Asia is a season of heavy rain between June and October following several dry months. It is unpredictable in duration and intensity.

## HURRICANES

Hurricanes, or typhoons, are frequent in South East Asia. These giant, spinning masses of wind and rain can cause much land devastation.

Regarded as one of the world's most beautiful buildings, the Taj Mahal, near Agra, India, was built in the 17th century as a tomb for an emperor's wife.

**The Taj Mahal**

**Mount Everest**

In the Himalayan range, Mount Everest is the highest point in the world at 8,847,73m. It is situated on the border of Nepal and Tibet.

# Arctic

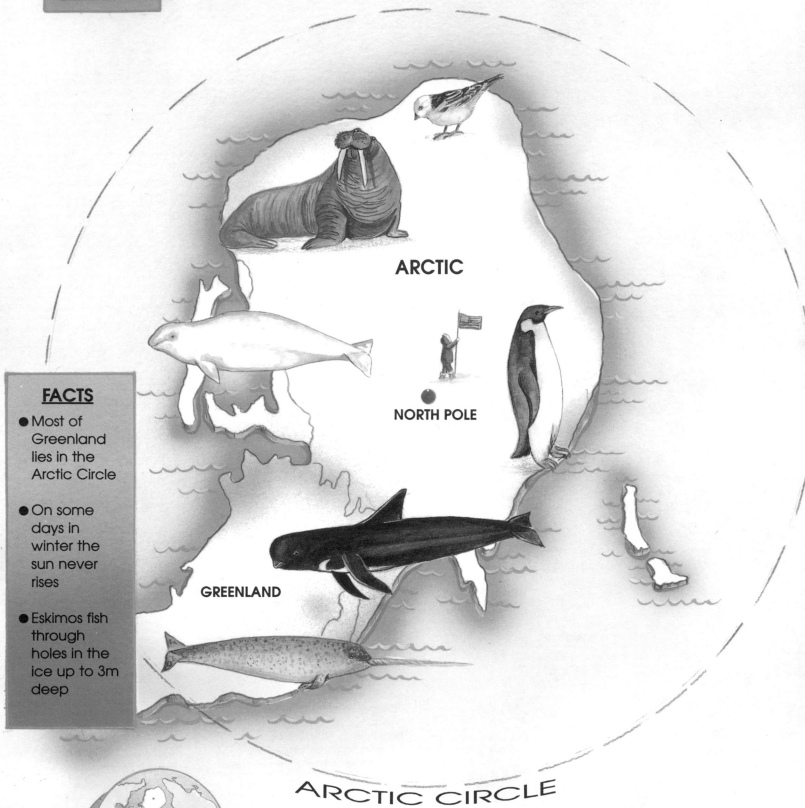

ARCTIC

NORTH POLE

GREENLAND

ARCTIC CIRCLE

## FACTS

● Most of Greenland lies in the Arctic Circle

● On some days in winter the sun never rises

● Eskimos fish through holes in the ice up to 3m deep

The Arctic is a region of sea surrounded by lands of Asia, Europe and North America. The sea around the North Pole is permanently frozen in winter and the surrounding land covered in snow and ice.

## ICE FLOWS

The flow of ice from land masses once summer approaches and surface snow and ice melt.

## SNOW FIELDS

Snow fields are large areas of permanent snow.

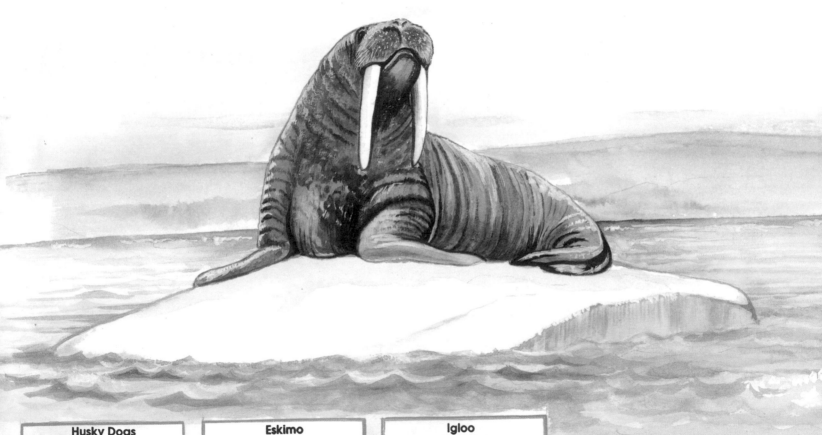

### Husky Dogs

Husky dogs are used in the Arctic to pull sledges which solves the constant problem of long distance transport.

### Eskimo

Eskimos inhabit the Arctic regions of North America and Greenland. They live in small family or tribal groups.

### Igloo

Eskimos live in igloos in the winter months. These snow huts form a base from which they fish and hunt.

# ANTARCTICA

southern Ocean

SOUTH POLE

ANTARCTICA

ANTARCTIC CIRCLE

South Pacific Ocean

## FACTS

- Antarctica covers an area of 5.5 million sq.miles

- Highest point is Vinson Massif at 5,140.14m

- The world's lowest recorded temperature was -89.2°C taken in 1983 at Vostok

Surrounding the South Pole, Antarctica was the last continent to be discovered. Doubtlessly Antarctica has the severest climate on earth and consequently there are no permanent inhabitants.

## GLACIERS

Slow moving masses of ice, glaciers originate from an accumulation of snow. When they reach the sea, huge chunks break off the ice face and icebergs float into the sea.

## EXPEDITIONS

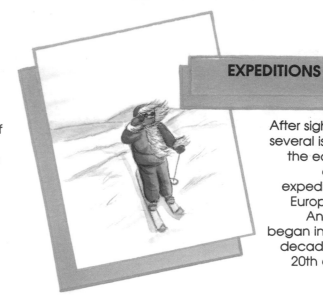

After sightings of several islands in the early 19th century, expeditions by Europeans to Antarctica began in the first decade of the 20th century.

### Scientist

Scientific research stations are the only human settlements on Antarctica. Research camps and weather stations are operated by several countries.

### Iceberg

Icebergs are floating masses of land ice. In Antarctica they are often 'calved' from an ice shelf.

### Icebreaker

Icebreakers are ships with a powerful bow which drive through ice exploring polar regions and maintaining shipping routes.

# TERRAIN

Ice and snow

Grassland

Broadleaf trees

Tundra and alpine

Desert

Needleleaf trees

High barren area

Dry scrub

Tropical rainforest

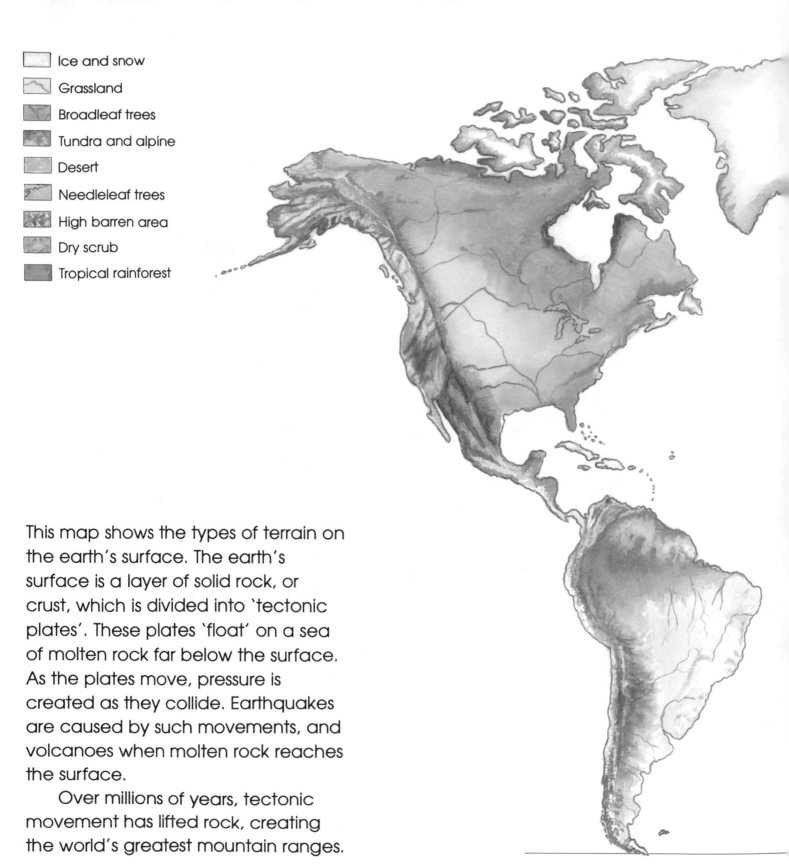

This map shows the types of terrain on the earth's surface. The earth's surface is a layer of solid rock, or crust, which is divided into 'tectonic plates'. These plates 'float' on a sea of molten rock far below the surface. As the plates move, pressure is created as they collide. Earthquakes are caused by such movements, and volcanoes when molten rock reaches the surface.

Over millions of years, tectonic movement has lifted rock, creating the world's greatest mountain ranges.

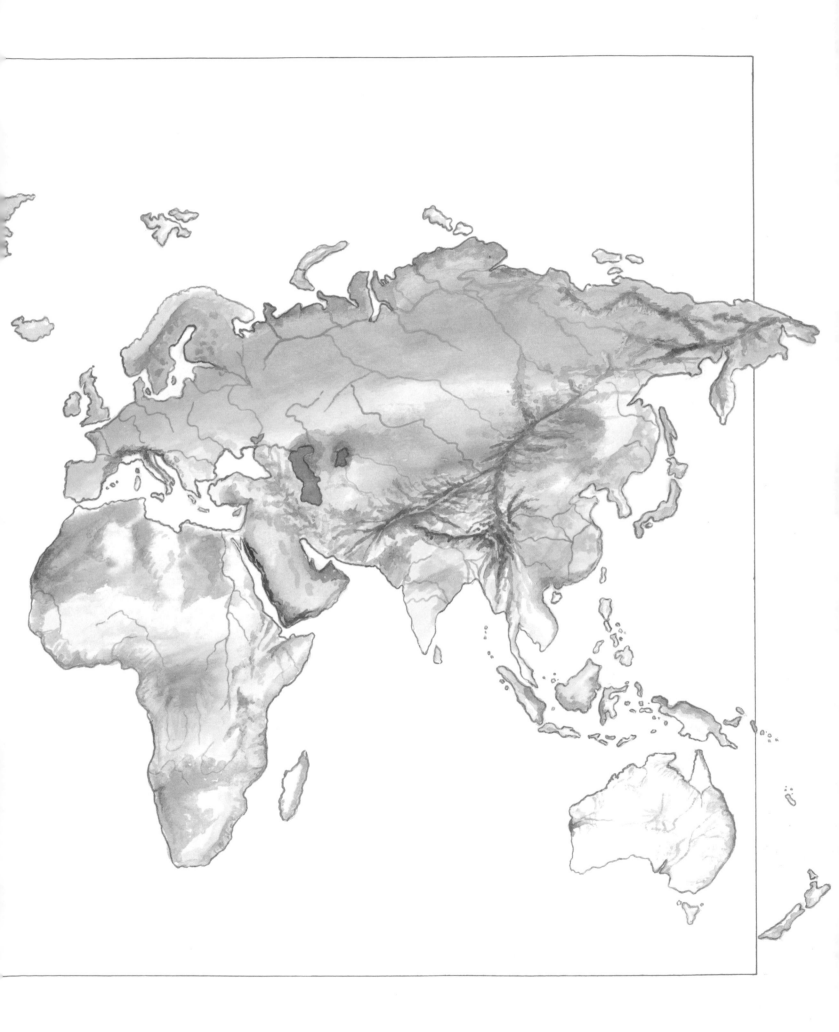

# CLIMATE

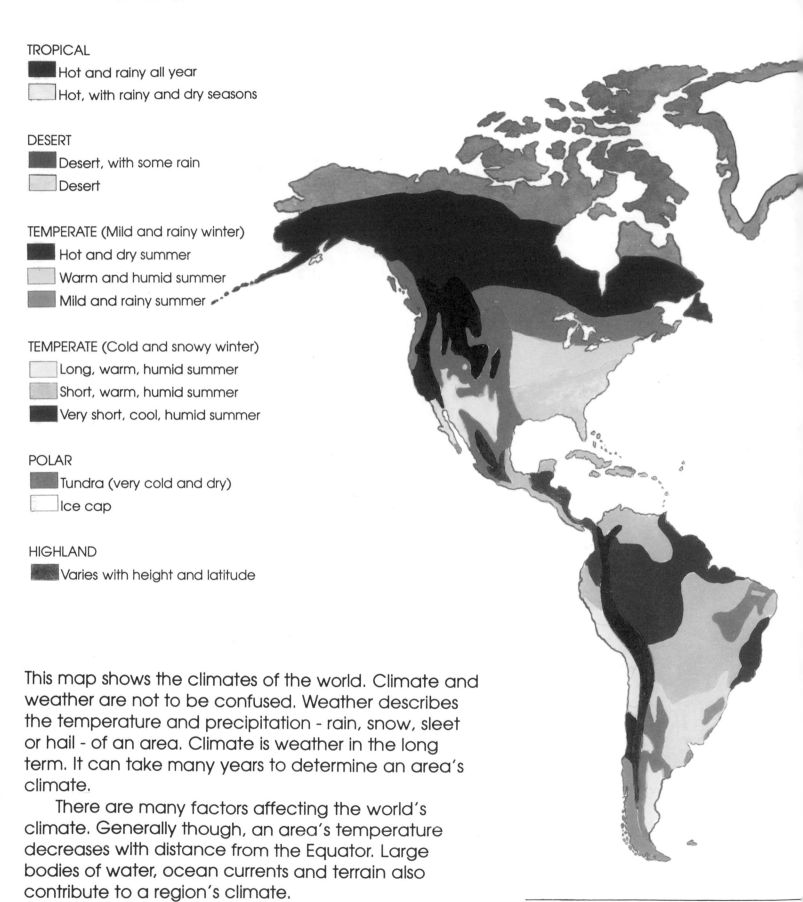

**TROPICAL**

■ Hot and rainy all year

□ Hot, with rainy and dry seasons

**DESERT**

■ Desert, with some rain

□ Desert

**TEMPERATE (Mild and rainy winter)**

■ Hot and dry summer

□ Warm and humid summer

■ Mild and rainy summer

**TEMPERATE (Cold and snowy winter)**

□ Long, warm, humid summer

□ Short, warm, humid summer

■ Very short, cool, humid summer

**POLAR**

■ Tundra (very cold and dry)

□ Ice cap

**HIGHLAND**

■ Varies with height and latitude

This map shows the climates of the world. Climate and weather are not to be confused. Weather describes the temperature and precipitation - rain, snow, sleet or hail - of an area. Climate is weather in the long term. It can take many years to determine an area's climate.

There are many factors affecting the world's climate. Generally though, an area's temperature decreases with distance from the Equator. Large bodies of water, ocean currents and terrain also contribute to a region's climate.